UMBRIA TO LOVE
Cuore d'Italia

photography by
Sandro Bellu

text by
Fedora Boco

EDITRICE LA ROCCA

EDITRICE

LA ROCCA

All rights reserved
Editrice La Rocca srl

Via XXIV Maggio, 71 - Marsciano - Perugia -
www.editricelarocca.it
info@editricelarocca.it
+39 075-8748170
+39 075 8741267

Photography by: Sandro Bellu
Text by: Fedora Boco
Edited by: Claudia Grisanti
Translation by: Marcus Daniel Mattia
Graphic design by: Alberto Hohenegger

Printed in July 2008 at:
Tipografia Petruzzi
Città di Castello

Agenzia di Promozione Turistica dell'Umbria
Palazzo Danzetta - Via Mazzini, 21
06121 Perugia
075.575951 - fax 075.5736828
info@apt.umbria.it
www.apt.umbria.it;
Sole Administrator of the
Agenzia di Promozione
Turistica dell'Umbria
Stefano Cimicchi

Cover Photo: The countryside around the town Giove

Index

Introduction

This concise yet rich guide illustrates minor and major sites of artistic beauty, some well known and others less so, marking a route divided into eight sections or itineraries: the Tiber Valley, Gubbio and its surroundings, Perugia and the Mid-Tiber Valley, Lake Trasimeno, the Valley of Umbria, Orvieto, Terni and the Valnerina.

The guide intends to develop knowledge and usability of a historical and artistic heritage of extraordinary quality in a setting and landscape which is both beautiful and precious.

This volume strengthens the image of Umbria through its history, culture, art and customs, addressing the interest not only of those wishing to know the area better, but above all that of the tourist, increasingly attentive and informed when visiting our region.

By means of exclusively commissioned high quality photographs accompanied by informative text, the guide intends to stimulate the traveller in search of new sensations and discoveries.

It is never possible to know a region well enough, for so numerous are its settlements – be they medium-sized, small or miniscule, each producing the images, layout and artistic qualities of cities. The result is that of an Umbria to be cherished, communicating its ancient charm in a new manner, and revealing a wealth of surprises.

Sole Administrator of the
Agenzia di Promozione Turistica dell'Umbria
Stefano Cimicchi

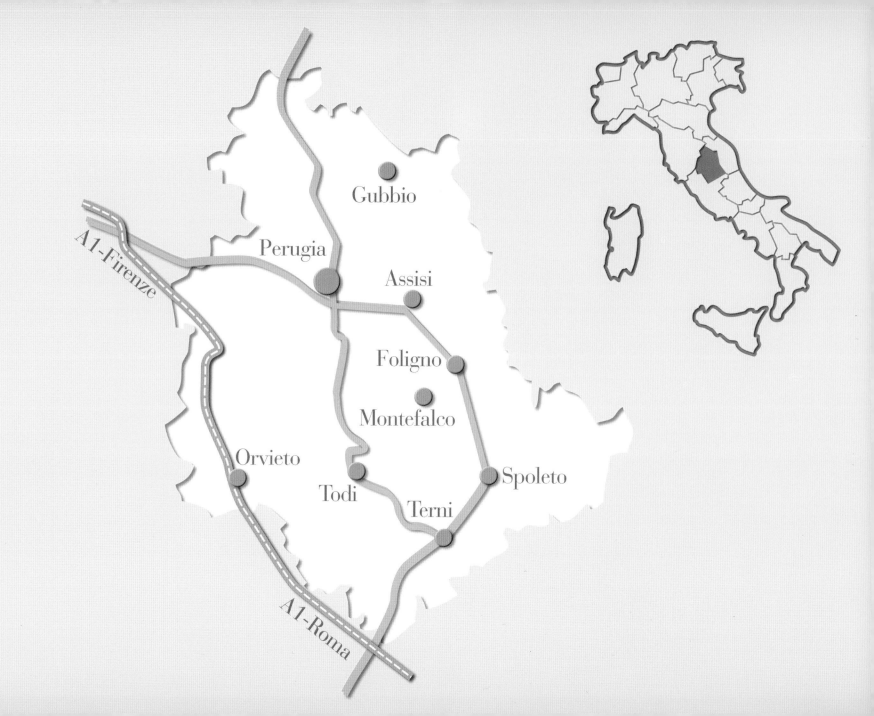

Gubbio

Perugia

Assisi

Foligno

Montefalco

A1-Firenze

Orvieto

Todi

Terni

Spoleto

A1-Roma

Sites in Umbria

Sandwiched between Tuscany, the Marches and Lazio, Umbria is a land which surprises, provokes strong emotions and captures the hearts of travellers. Boasting an extraordinary variety of landscapes and partly dominated by the splendour of its 13th and 14th century architecture, it is positioned in the centre of the Italian peninsula – the heart of central Italy. Indeed, the exact geographical centre of mainland Italy can be found near the town of Narni. This condition has historically guaranteed that the region had always been a crossroads of people and diverse cultures, at times conflicting, yet always a source of exchanges of ideas and experiences. Umbria houses the testimony of a culture whose origins are thousands of years old, expressed through history, art and the popular traditions of people who have lived on this land since the earliest recorded times: from the original Umbrians to the Etruscans, the ancient Romans and Longobards, up to the time of the Papal State. Every church, square and alleyway, down to the very stones of the towns and villages tell the story of this glorious region. In many settlements we can find museums and art galleries of various sizes and contents, each proudly safeguarding authentic artistic masterpieces from all periods of time.

One particular characteristic of Umbria is the natural beauty of its landscape combined with its modern economy and road systems, where the tourist can find a decidedly satisfactory range of choices. Its surface area of 8,456 km² (of which 53% is categorised as mountainous, 41% as hilly and only 6% as plain) is inhabited by just over 870,000 people.

It is a wonderful place both to live in and to visit: the ideal destination for an unforgettable holiday. The opportunities for touring around and staying in different places are huge, as Umbria can offer such a great variety of solutions, from ancient convents and rustic farmhouses to refurbished castles and abbeys, and of course high quality hotels. A natural destination for travellers seeking peace and quiet, it is also home to numerous events of great importance – the Umbria Jazz festival in Perugia, Terni and Orvieto, the Festival of the Two Worlds in Spoleto, Trasimeno Blues Festival, the Cinema Festival of Narni, the 'Sagra Musicale Umbra' Classical music event in Perugia, the Festival of Nations Chamber Music Festival in Città di Castello, the Giostra della Quintana in Foligno – events which animate the region's towns and villages all year round and make Umbria a variegated stage. Other events of major interest include the Todiarte Festival, the season of classical plays at the Roman theatre in Gubbio, the Segni Barocchi Festival in Foligno and more. A wealth of aesthetic and cultural temptations, as well as faithful guardian of ancient traditions. Other irresistible temptations are those of the palate: in the region's numerous farmhouses, bistros and restaurants it is possible to taste deliciously simple and genuine dishes prepared today in the same way as in times of old.

The Upper Tiber Valley

Città di Castello

Built on a slight plain (288m above sea level) among pleasant rolling, green hills, this is the most important and populated town of the Upper-Tiber Valley. Still surrounded in part by its 16th century walls, the town boasts charming ancient monuments and numerous high quality events attracting thousands of visitors every year. In the 15th and 16th centuries Città di Castello was an important crossroads for the Arts, open to diverse influences from Tuscany, the Marches and Rome, and to this day it conserves a strong cultural tradition, nourished by the contributions of artists such as Luca Signorelli, Raffaello (who painted four of his masterpieces here), Vasari, Rosso Fiorentino and the contemporary painter Alberto Burri, who in 1982 and 1990 donated to the town an outstanding collection of his works, which is today on show in the two sites of Palazzo Albizzini (via Albizzini 1) and the former tobacco factories in via Pierucci, offering the greatest existing documentation of the artist's entire output. The municipal Art Gallery is housed in the 16th century palazzo Vitelli alla Cannoniera, and boasts paintings by Spinello Aretino and Luca Signorelli, terracotta work by Andrea and Luca Della Robbia, besides the Gonfalone della Santissima Trinità (1501-1502) by the young Raffaello. The Museo del Capitolo, entirely restructured, consists of an important collection of sacred and cult objects and of extremely refined jewellery including an altar frontal, a crosier and a rare collection of 7th century trays and spoons used for Holy Communion and rediscovered in Canoscio in 1935. The cult of the arts in Città di Castello is similarly evident in the continuing practice of artisan crafts which to this day still use ancient manufacturing processes, foremost of which are weaving and printing.

Città di Castello. Panorama.

Città di Castello. The cylindrical bell tower of the Cathedral.

Città di Castello. Panorama from the Municipal tower with the church of San Francesco (1273)

Città di Castello. Portal of the left side of the Cathedral, detail of the decoration dating back to the XIV century reconstruction.

Città di Castello. Facade of the Cathedral. Named after the saints Florido and Amanzio, it was built in the XI century, extended in 1356 and almost completely renovated between 1466 and 1529. In the background we can see the high tower of the town hall.

Città di Castello. Palazzo Vitelli alla Cannoniera. Detail of the decoration in graffiti executed in 1532-34 by Cristoforo Gherardi probably on an idea by Giorgio Vasari. The building houses the Municipal Art Gallery.

Città di Castello. Alberto Burri, Metamorfotex, 1991. One of 128 works, subdivided into cycles, created between 1974 and 1993 and today housed in the former tobacco drying factory. The great warehouses, built in the '50s and '60s for the drying of tropical tobacco produced in the area and painted entirely in black following the wishes of the artist, have housed the Alberto Burri Collection since 1990.

Monte Santa Maria Tiberina, mid-XIII century fortress of the marquises of the Monte. Panorama.

Monte Santa Maria Tiberina. Panorama over the Upper Tiber Valley.

Montone, Municipal Museum. Bartolomeo Caporali, Gonfalone della Madonna del Soccorso, 1481. The details feature the village of Montone with the Fortress constructed by Braccio Fortebraccio.

San Giustino. Castello Bufalini, constructed between 1480 and 1492 as a military fortress, transformed in the XVI Century into a genteel residence. In 1998 it was acquired by the State to be used as a Museum.

A·D·M·CCCC·LXXXII
OP : m : CONVENTVS

Montone.
Panorama. The
village, ellipsoidal
in shape, is
enclosed by the
original medieval
walls.

Montone. The
fortress of Aries.
Once belonging
to the
Fortebraccio
family, this was
the first fortified
settlement in
Montone.

Umbertide (in ancient times Pitulum, later Fratta). Panorama of the historical centre with a row of ancient looking houses and the bridge over the Reggia stream.

Umbertide. The beautiful castle of Civitella Ranieri, splendid example of a medieval fortress, was constructed shortly after the year 1000. Rebuilt in the XV century, it has a square plan with large cylindrical towers at the corners and a big donjon.

The area of Gubbio and Gualdo

Countryside in the area around Sigillo.

Gubbio

At 522 m above sea level, Gubbio is an ancient Umbrian town situated at the foot of Mount Ingino, rich in monuments testifying to its glorious past. Evidence of the town's ancient origins can be found in the seven 'Tavole Eugubine' (Tables of Gubbio), one of the most important Italic documents, today preserved in the Palazzo dei Consoli, and in the Roman Theatre situated just outside the town walls. Architecturally, Gubbio is the absolute masterpiece of medieval civilisation. From the 14th century the town was in the hands of the Montefeltro Dukes of Urbino who ruled there until 1508, the year in which the Della Rovere family succeeded them. The domination of the Dukes and Counts of Urbino gave place to a period of civil and artistic flourishing. Dominated from above by the monumental Basilica of Sant'Ubaldo which safeguards the intact remains of its patron, Gubbio houses architectural masterpieces evoking the power of this medieval city-state (Palazzo dei Consoli for example), while the Palazzo Ducale is a typical Renaissance building commissioned by Federico di Montefeltro and proposing, in a smaller form, architectural solutions identical to those used in the Palazzo Ducale in Urbino itself. During the 16th century Gubbio saw an outstanding period of artistic expression coinciding with the development of ceramics, which was taken to the highest level by the master Giorgio Andreoli and his descendants. In the Municipal Museum it is today possible to admire part of the Master's output alongside illustrious examples of 14th century majolica work. Among the most important events organised by the city the most noteworthy are the Corsa dei Ceri and the historical re-enactment of the Palio della Balestra. Gubbio is ever increasingly a destination for high quality tourism.

Gubbio. Palazzo dei Consoli, the spiral staircase to the Gothic entrance portal.

Gubbio. Palazzo dei Consoli, one of the most important examples of civil Italian architecture, constructed between 1332 and 1349. Today it is the home of the Art Gallery and the Archaeological Museum, which conserves the 'Tavole Eugubine' (the Tables of Gubbio), the most important document in the history of the Italic people.

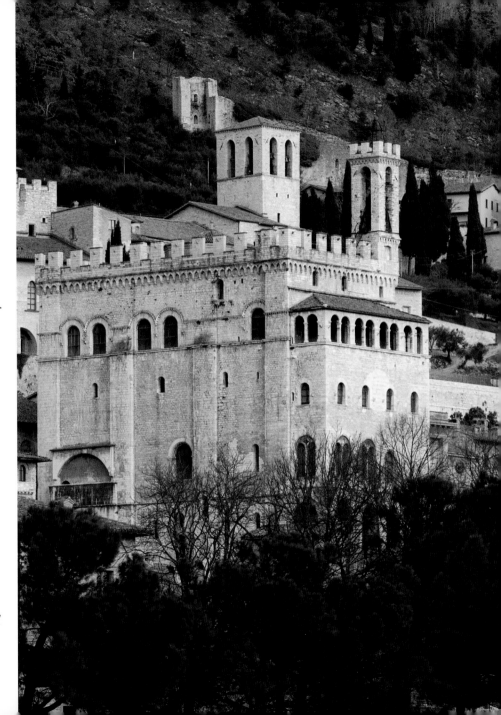

The 'corsa dei ceri' along the streets of Gubbio. This takes place on 15th May every year, the day before the death (in 1160) of the patron saint Ubaldo, and is a centuries-old tradition. The event is characterised by three gigantic wooden staffs, on top of which are perched the statues of Saint Ubaldo, Saint George and Saint Anthony, and which are carried on the shoulders of robust men, in a frenetic race through the streets of the town to Mount Ingino.

Gubbio, Campanella (14th -15th)

Gubbio. The XV Century 'Palazzo del Bargello' and the Fountain of the Madmen, named so because of a tradition whereby running round it three times and wetting oneself with its water confers the licence of "madman".

Gualdo Tadino. View of the town with the bell tower of the Basilica of San Benedetto (1256), the main church of the town of Gualdo which stands in the main square.

32

Perugia and the Mid-Tiber Valley

Perugia. Spring in the area of Madonna del Piano

Perugia

At 493 m above sea level, Perugia is a very ancient Umbrian town stretched out over a hillside acropolis. Today it has over 162.000 inhabitants and is the provincial and regional capital of the area. It is 176 km from Rome and 158 from Florence. A city of art, Perugia is a popular destination for numerous tourists who come to enjoy its abundant artistic and cultural heritage: the National Gallery of Umbria, with works from the schools of Umbria and Siena, by Taddeo di Bartolo, Gentile da Fabriano, Benozzo Gozzoli, Angelico, Piero della Francesca, Bonfigli, Caporali, the Perugino, Pintoricchio, Spagna and more; the Collegio del Cambio (a vast decorative work produced by Perugino between 1498 and 1500), the Collegio della Mercanzia and the Archeological Museum, housing highly important collections of prehistoric and Etruscan-Roman Art. Among the most significant finds is the Cippo of Perugia, a travertine block with a long etching in the Etruscan language. The city also possesses two perimeter walls: the Etruscan walls built between the IV and III centuries B.C. and the medieval walls incorporating the villages which had subsequently developed around the ancient Etruscan gates (the Etruscan Arch, Porta Marzia, Porta Trasimena, Arco dei Gigli, Arco della Mandorla or Porta Eburnea, Arco di Sant'Ercolano or Porta Cornea). Perugia is also home to an ancient University founded in 1308, as well as the largest University for Foreigners in Italy. Today it is a modern city well known throughout the world for its numerous cultural events (Umbria Jazz – International Festival of Jazz Music and the 'Sagra Musicale Umbra' Classical Music event). Perugia is also an innovative city in the field of public transport: it was the first Italian city to construct escalators in various places around the town, in order to make the centre accessible on foot. Furthermore, the city has recently completed a light over ground metropolitan system known as the Minimetrò. The regional airport of Sant'Egidio, 12 km away, operates daily connections with the north of the country and other European cities.

Perugia. Palazzo dei Priori in Piazza IV Novembre (also known as Piazza Grande).

Perugia. Tower of the Palazzo dei Priori, superb expression of the communal spirit of the city; it was erected between the XIII and XV centuries.

Perugia. Fontana Maggiore (1275-1278). One of the main monuments of the city and of the entire sculptural output of medieval times. Designed by Frà Bevignate, it is made up of two concentric polygon marble basins surmounted by a bronze cup. The two basins are decorated with bas-relief exquisitely sculpted by Nicola and Giovanni Pisano. The lower basin includes 50 mirrors with bas-relief of the allegories of the months and the sciences, episodes from sacred and Roman history , and from Esops fables. The upper basin consists of 24 smooth mirrors, separated by the same number of small statues depicting saints, the virtues, and historical characters. The bowl is surmounted by a bronze group of three nymphs. It underwent long and laborious restoration work in 1997.

Perugia. The Braccio Lodges (1423), monument of the Proto Renaissance in Perugia attributed to Fioravante Fioravanti from Bologna, they lean against the Cathedral wall.

Perugia. Bell tower of Santa Giuliana, one of few in the city conserving the Gothic cusp.

Perugia. The minimetro, a new system of public transport connecting the historical centre with the area called Pian di Massiano along the north-south axis of the city.

Perugia. The minimetro. In the background the medieval Tower of the Sciri.

Perugia. Via Appia, ancient acqueduct built during the second half of the 13th Century, enabling water to be brought from Mount Pacciano to the famous fountain in Piazza IV Novembre.

Perugia. Temple of San Michele Arcangelo. Building with a central plan dating to the 5th or 6th Century.

Perugia. Church of San Pietro, interior consisting of a nave and two choir stalls. It houses the largest Art collection in Perugia after the National Gallery of Umbria. The nave is made up of arches on ancient grey marble columns. The upper part is decorated with canvasses depicting scenes from the Old and New Testaments.

CEDERE CVNTA MEIS PVLSA
ET DISIECTA LACERTIS
MAGNA SATIS FVERINT
TRES DOCVMENTA VIRI
NIL EGO PRO PATRIA TIMEO
CHARISQVE PROPINQVIS
QVAEQVE ALIOS TERRET
MORS MIHI GRATA VENIT

DIC DEA QVAE TIBI VIS MO
RES REGO PECTORIS AESTVS
TEMPERO ET VIS ALIOS
CVM VOLO REDDO PARES
ME SEQVERE ET QVA TE SV
PERES RATIONE DOCEBO
QVID TV QVOD VALLAS
VINCERE MAIVS ERIT

LVTIO SICINIO · LEONIDA LACEDEMONIO · ORATIO COCLES · PVBLIO SCIPIONE · PERICLES ATHENIESE · QVINTO CINCINNATO

Perugia. Collegio del Cambio, interior. Sala dell'Udienza with frescoes by Perugino (1498-1500) adorning the walls and the ogival vaults.

Perugia. Etruscan Arch. Also known as the Augustan Arch, it is the best preserved and most monumental of the Etruscan gates of the city. Built in the second half of the III century B.C., it consists of a facade traversed by one single opening and by two trapezoidal turrets.

AVGVSTA PERVSIA MCCCCLXI

Perugia. Church of San Bernardino in Piazza San Francesco al Prato. The polychromic facade is the work of the Florentine Agostino di Antonio di Duccio (1457-1461).

Perugia. Bell tower of the Church of Santa Maria Nuova erected in 1644, possibly planned by Galeazzo Alessi.

Perugia. Detail of the façade of San Bernardino

*Torgiano. Museum of Wine.
Inside the 18th century 'palazzo
Graziani-Baglioni' the museum is
a fascinating testimony to the
theme of grapes and the culture
of wine production (from
archaeological finds to XX
century examples).*

*Bettona, one of the most
beautiful villages in the whole of
Italy. Panorama.*

54

Deruta

Is situated 15 km to the south of Perugia on a hill dominating the Tiber Valley. Of the old castle of the town several parts of the walls remain, as well as the arches of the three entrance gates and the characteristic medieval lanes which lead to the Piazza dei Consoli and the 'palazzo' of the same name, today the home of the Town hall, with its 14th century tower adorned with Romanic mullioned windows. The Art Gallery is certainly worth visiting, boasting highly valuable paintings from different ages, as is the Museum of Ceramics which houses some extremely refined examples of the town's ceramics production from the XIV to the XX centuries.

Deruta. Regional Museum of Ceramics. This collection, which was started by Francesco Briganti at the end of the XIX century to document the origins and history of the ceramics tradition in Deruta, has been subsequently enriched, since the 1980s, by new acquisitions illustrating production from Medieval times until 1930.

Todi.

In a high position dominating the Tiber Valley, Todi (400m above s.l.) developed in three successive periods, each testified by a circle of walls: pre-Roman, Roman and medieval. From the first half of the 13th century the town itself was divided into six districts (Nidola, Colle, Valle, Santa Prassede, San Silvestro and Santa Maria in Camuccia), while the entire municipal territory was divided into 37 parts. The piazza Grande or Maggiore is the heart of the historical centre. The various buildings that look onto the square are the Palazzo del Popolo, Palazzo del Podestà or Palace of Justice, Palazzo dei Priori and the cathedral preceded by an 18th century flight of steps. Not far from the square is the church of San Fortunato, patron of the town, for centuries the home of minor Francescan monks, one of whom was Jacopone. Todi offers a highly regarded series of cultural initiatives such as the Italian Antiques Fair which is usually held in Spring.

Todi. Church of Santa Maria della Consolazione, one of the most important buildings of the Umbrian Renaissance, the plans of which are traditionally attributed to Bramante. It was constructed between 1508 and 1607

Todi. Church of San Fortunato, constructed between 1292 and as late as the XV century. The facade, the upper part of which has remained unfinished, was built between 1415 and 1458 by Giovanni di Santuccio of Fiorenzuola, assisted by his nephew Bartolo di Angelo. The centrepiece of the composition is the greater portal (1424-36), a pointed arch decorated with small spiral columns and sculptures attributed to the circle of Jacopo della Quercia.

Todi. Church of San Fortunato, interior. Detail of the pedestal of a column.

Todi. Panorama at dusk.

Todi. The magnificent central rose window,12th - 14th

The countryside around Todi.

Gualdo Cattaneo, Internal lane of the medieval village fortified by Barattano.

Villa San Faustino. Benedectine Abbey of San Faustino.

*Montecchio, parish church of
Santa Maria of Romanic origin.*

*Massa Martana. Church of Santa
Maria in Pantano, one of the
oldest in Umbria, built in the
traditional style by San Severo.*

Lake Trasimeno

Lake Trasimeno in spring.

Lake Trasimeno

Enclosed by soft rolling hills, is the fourth largest lake in Italy. It is of tectonic origin and is fed principally by rainfall and a few streams. It is without outlets. The surface area of its basin is approx. 128 Km^2 with a depth no greater than six metres. On the lake there are three islands: Maggiore (the only which is inhabited), Minore and Polvese (which strangely enough is larger than Maggiore despite the latter's name). The local fauna is extraordinarily rich, and includes pike, carp, tench, eel and barbel. Positioned on the border between Umbria and Tuscany, Lake Trasimeno is at the centre of one of the areas of greatest historic, artistic and cultural wealth in the whole country, not forgetting its strong local traditions. Two thousand years of history surround this lake. In the radius of a mere 100km we can find 20% of the artistic heritage of the entire world: Florence, Perugia, Siena, Arezzo, Assisi, Orvieto, Gubbio, Spoleto, Chiusi, Cortona and Tarquinia. Furthermore, within reach are the most important centres of Renaissance Art in Italy, as well as a considerable part of ancient and medieval art. The most interesting places to visit along the lake are Castiglion del Lago, Magione, Paciano, Panicale, Passignano, Piegaro, Tuoro and Città della Pieve, this last being notable as the birthplace, in 1448, of Pietro Vannucci, better known as the Perugino. There are numerous artistic accounts of the painter's presence in the town: the beautiful *Adorazione dei Magi* (1504) in the oratory of Santa Maria dei Bianchi and the *Deposizione dalla Croce* (1517) at Santa Maria dei Servi.

Lake Trasimeno, the fourth largest lake in Italy.

Magione. Castle of the Knights of Malta, courtyard with three lodges, from the 15th Century.

View of Monte del Lago

Tuoro sul Trasimeno. Campo del Sole. An architectural group of sculptures in "serena" stone, typical of the area, in Punta Navaccia, by the Lido di Tuoro. It was produced through the work of 28 sculptors over a period of five years (1985-1989). The project is in the form of a great spiral flask sketched by 27 columns-sculptures leading to a central panel, surmounted by a solar symbol.

Castiglion del Lago. Palazzo della Corgna, interior. The dwelling of a wealthy aristocrat started by Ascanio della Corgna in 1563 on plans by Galeazzo Alessi, a noted architect from Perugia. The series of frescoes adorning the rooms, covering a surface of over 1.200 m² on the main floor, is a valuable testimony of late Mannerism in Umbria (Niccolò Circignani aka il Pomarancio, Gian Antonio Pandolfi, Salvio Savini).

Città della Pieve. Oratory of Santa Maria dei Bianchi, fresco by Pietro Perugino with the Natività (1504).

A·D·M·D·IIII

Città della Pieve. Panorama.

Panicale. Cesare Caporali Theatre. A little architectural gem from the first half of the 18th century, seating 154, with a horseshoe structure, decorated entirely in stucco.

Corciano

At 408 m above sea level, Corciano is a typical medieval castle in a perfect state of repair, since the year 2003 it has been included in the list of the 'most beautiful villages in Italy', and is situated only 12 km from Perugia and 10 km from Lake Trasimeno. Today still surrounded by robust walls, Corciano overlooks numerous castles and medieval lookout towers arranged in an amphitheatre around Monte Malbe (652 m above sea level) and which today constitute the seven outlying divisions of the municipal territory: Capocavallo, Castelvieto, Chiugiana, Mantignana, Figiana, San Mariano and Solomeo. Roaming through its streets we can admire, besides the numerous churches, Piazza dei Caduti, the 16th century Town Hall, the 15th century Palazzo del Capitano del Popolo, Palazzo dei Priori e della Mercanzia, Piazza Coragino, the Municipal Tower.

Corciano. One of the most important castles of the countryside of Perugia, according to documents dating back to the XII century. The ancient centre, standing over the modern development, maintains intact the medieval plan of the 'Castro'.

Corciano. Panorama.

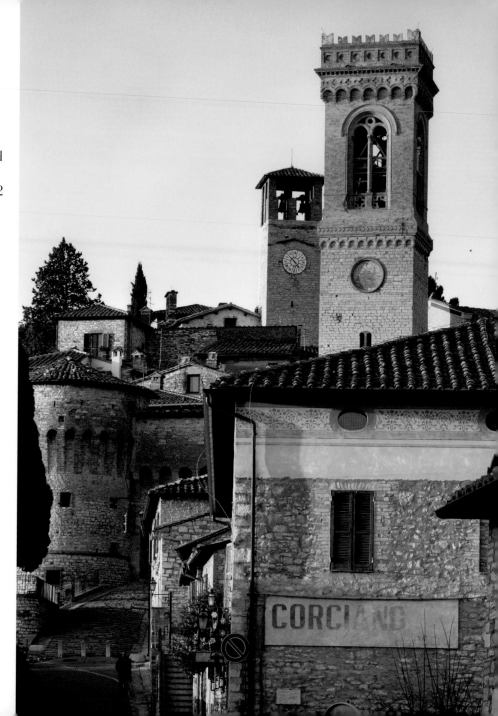

The Valley of Umbria

Surroundings of Bevagna with the Sagrantino vineyards.

Assisi

Spreading over the Western slopes of Mount Subasio, at 424 m above sea level Assisi dominates an extremely fertile plane at the centre of which stands out the basilica of Santa Maria degli Angeli. The entire town of Assisi is enclosed in a broad circle of medieval walls with the Rocca Maggiore towering over them, and to the East, the Rocca Minore or Rocchicciola. The "city of San Francesco" is rich in monuments which are exceptional both for their architecture and their figurative art (the Basilica of San Francesco, San Pietro, the Basilica of Santa Chiara, the Cathedral of San Rufino). In Via Ancajani 3 there is a Gallery of Contemporary Art housing important works by contemporary Italian and foreign painters who were each inspired by sacred art (De Chirico, Greco, Rosai, Fazzini, Pirandello).

Santa Maria degli Angeli. General view with the Basilica in the foreground.

Assisi. Basilica of San Francesco, one of the most important temples in the Christian world. Made up of two superimposed churches, it was started in July 1228, two years after the death of the Saint. The Basilica would later become the cradle of Modern Art at the time thanks to the contributions of artists such as Cimabue, Giotto, Pietro Lorenzetti and Simone Martini. The Basilica of San Francesco in Assisi also marked the appearance of Gothic architecture in the region, which would subsequently find its most supreme expression in the Cathedral of Orvieto.

Assisi. In the Upper Church the walls of the nave are decorated in the famous cycle of frescoes attributed no longer to Giotto but to the workshop of Pietro Cavallini, painted from 1277 onwards, and illustrating moments of the life of San Francesco.

Assisi. Temple of Minerva, one of the best preserved monuments of the Classical world. Dating back to the first centuries of the Empire, in 1539 it was transformed into a church entitled Santa Maria sopra Minerva.

Assisi. Basilica of Santa Chiara. Initiated in 1257, as early as 1260 the body of the saint was transferred here. The building has a simple façade of horizontal white and red rows in local stone, divided into three zones by cornices. Above the portal can be seen an exquisitely elegant rose window with two rounds of small columns and arches.

Assisi. The Rocca Maggiore. Ancient residence of Federico II of Svevia, it was demolished in 1198 by the people of Assisi and reconstructed in 1367 by Albornoz.

Santa Maria degli Angeli. The Porziuncola where Francesco d'Assisi died on 3 October 1226. Situated inside the Basilica of Santa Maria degli Angeli, it conserves to this day the 14th century structure including the roof in white and pink marble. The fresco on the facade is by the Nazarene painter Friedrich Overbeck (1829).

Spello

Situated 34 km from Perugia and 165 km from Rome, Spello is among
the most interesting towns in Umbria. It offers one of the most
beautiful and breathtaking views from a natural and urban point of
view in the whole region, situated as it is on a narrow spur of Mount
Subasio overlooking the Valley of Umbria. The original character of
the early Roman town continues to exist, revised in medieval times.
Clinging to the eastern side of the mountain are the medieval villages
of Collepino and San Giovanni. Inside the town walls of Spello there
are numerous stopping points on the way to the main square: Piazza
del Belvedere, the town's highest point from which the panorama over
the Valley of Umbria can be admired. Among the monuments which
should not be missed are the collegiate church of Santa Maria
Maggiore, present already in 1025, completely transformed in the mid-
XVII century, and containing, on the left, the Baglioni Chapel (aka
Cappella Bella), with its notable cycle of frescoes by Bernardino di
Betto, the Pintoricchio, produced between 1500 and 1503,
commissioned by Troilo Baglioni.

*Spello. Panorama. The medieval
centre of the town, situated on a
narrow extension of Mount
Subasio, overlooking the Valley of
Umbria, has preserved intact the
ancient network of roads and
buildings.*

Spello. Porta Venere. Beautiful construction in travertine dating back to Augustan times. It opens with three passages, the central one reserved to vehicles and the lateral ones to pedestrians. In Medieval times it was flanked by two polygonal turrets.

Bevagna

The ancient Roman *Mevania* is 35 km from Perugia and 148 from Rome. Within its walls it preserves the overriding appearance of a medieval town where traditional artisan trades are still flourishing, with their workshops opening onto the characteristic lanes, the monuments and, above all, the splendid square, boasting all the main religious and civil buildings of the town. Friezes, mosaics and Roman columns add value to the town, which houses the testimony of its own history. The settlement of the ancient Roman *Mevania* coincides almost entirely with that of the medieval and modern town. In recent times urban development has extended beyond the walls, to the area where once part of the Roman town was to be found, and where some important discoveries have been made.

The Civic Museum with its rich archaeological collection is well worth a visit. The Palazzo dei Consoli is also highly interesting. Alongside the three Romanic churches occupying the square, it helps make Piazza Silvestri among the most beautiful in the entire region. During the first two weeks of June every year Bevagna hosts the Mercato delle Gaite, a particular event in which products and handmade articles are created following ancient techniques in old workshops revived for the occasion: including candles, ropes, fabrics, silk, paper, wicker baskets, ironwork, vases, copper work and much more.

Bevagna. Piazza Silvestri (entomologist from Bevagna, 1873-1949).

Bevagna. Church of San Michele Arcangelo, detail. The church was constructed between the end of the XII century and the beginning of the XIII by the masters Binello and Rodolfo, whose names are remembered in an inscription on the left of the portal.

Bevagna. Panorama.

Foligno

At 234m above sea level, Foligno is the third largest town in Umbria, and is in the province of Perugia. It is a town built on a plain crossed by the river Topino which has filled a connecting role between the two seas: the Tyrrhenian and the Adriatic, described as a commercial pole. According to an ancient tradition Foligno was considered the "centre of the World". It is in fact in the very centre of the Italian peninsula, which is itself a country in the centre of Europe, and more importantly of the Mediterranean Sea which, in ancient times was considered the centre of the World, as its name suggests. The history of the town is one of numerous earthquakes, the most recent being on 26 September 1997, causing very serious damage to both the city and its mountainous outskirts. The municipal Art Gallery in palazzo Trinci (on the Northern side of the piazza della Repubblica) contains a rich heritage documenting both Umbrian painting in general and that of Foligno in particular, especially the period between the XIV and XVI centuries with works by Alunno, his son Lattanzio, and his master Pier Antonio Mezzastris; and frescoes by Bartolomeo di Tommaso and Giovanni di Corraduccio. It is well worth visiting.

Foligno. Panorama of the town surrounded by the medieval walls erected beside the River Topino.

Foligno. Cathedral, detail of the portal, the work of the masters Rodolfo and Binello (1201). The carved wooden door is from 1620.

Abbey di Sassovivo. view of the cloister.

Marshes of
Colfiorito, form of
ecosystem of
exceptional
importance due
to the rare plant
and animal
species

Abbey of
Sassovivo
immersed in a
solitary wooded
landscape.
Founded in the
second half of the
XI century
reutilising a pre-
existent fortified
residence, today it
houses the Jesus
Caritas
Community of
Padre Foucauld

Montefalco

At 473m above sea level, Montefalco is called the "Banister of Umbria" because of its surprising panoramic view, due to its dominant position overlooking the valleys of the Topino and the Clitunno. Inside its ancient walls it houses monuments of great importance from various ages such as the Town Hall, of 13th century origins (1270), the Church of Sant'Agostino (1269-1285), the Romanic church of San Bartolomeo, with the nearby gate of Federico II from 1244 recalling his stay in Montefalco, and the church of Santa Chiara, which houses paintings from the Umbrian school. In the first decades of the XIV century construction work on the church of San Francesco was begun. It is now the Civic Museum, and houses the highly famous cycle of "Stories of San Francesco" painted by the Florentine painter Benozzo Gozzoli in 1451-52, frescoes and panels from the Umbrian school in the XIV and XV centuries, by Pietro Vannucci, Antoniazzo Romano, the workshop of Melozzo da Forlì, Nicolò Alunno and Francesco Melanzio. Montefalco is well-known also from the manufacturing of linen, cotton and hemp fabric with Greek key designs which, in their colours and forms, renew an ancient tradition. Besides its high quality olive oil, this land is also responsible for another world-famous product: the Sagrantino D.O.C.G. and Rosso Montefalco D.O.C. wines.

Plateau of Colfiorito.

Montefalco. Panorama.

Montefalco. Church of Sant'Agostino constructed between 1279 and 1285. Fresco with the Natività (XV C).

Surroundings of Montefalco with olive groves.

Trevi, panorama. Situated on a hill dominating the Valley of Umbria, the town, in which the ancient paving of the roads continues to exist, has preserved the appearance of the medieval village.

Castello di Pissignano, typical example of a sloping castle with a triangular plan still conserving intact the perimeter of its walls, intersected by impressive polygonal towers and two gate-towers.

On the Via Flaminia stands the elegant Tempietto del Clitunno (or Church of San Salvatore), erected between the IV-V century A.D. over a pre-existent pagan construction. The building is constructed mainly with material recovered from ancient Rome and is composed of two superimposed rooms. The facade "in antis", constructed in regular rows of chalk conchs, includes a portico with four columns, of which the two most central are foliate and the two lateral are spirals leaning against fluted pillars.

Spoleto

At 396 m above sea level, Spoleto is one of the main tourist centres of Umbria, and internationally famous. The reasons for this success are traceable to the great historical, artistic, cultural and naturalistic heritage offered by the town and its territory. Positioned on the Sant' Elia hill at the foot of Monteluco, on the banks of the Tessino stream, at the lower end of the Umbrian Valley, Spoleto is an ancient settlement dating back to prehistory. The Rocca (1.200 m², two thirds of which are used as a museum), positioned on the summit of the hill, was started in 1359, commissioned by the cardinal Egidio Albornoz, who wished to make here one of the strongest points of support in the dominion of the Pope, recently returned from captivity in Avignon. Recently it underwent important restoration work (lasting 14 years) and which was concluded with the setting up of the National Museum of the Duchy of Spoleto. It consists of fifteen exhibition rooms spread over two floors, 190 works on display testifying a thousand years of history from the middle of the 4thcentury until the end of the 15th century. In Piazza del Duomo we find the small and elegant Caio Melisso Theatre, started in 1664 and completely renovated by Giovanni Montiroli in 1880 with a curtain by Domenico Bruschi, and the cathedral itself built in Romanic style towards the end of the XII century with a facade divided horizontally into three orders: in the lower order we find the magnificent Romanic portal. To the left of the facade is the mighty bell tower constructed in the XII century with material coming from Roman, Paleo- Christian and alto-medieval remains. The apse of the Cathedral was decorated by the Florentine artist Filippo Lippi. Lovers of contemporary art will wish to visit the Civic Gallery of Modern Art in the splendid premises of Palazzo Collicola, ancient town residence of the noble Collicola family. The Festival dei Due Mondi (also known as the Spoleto Festival) founded in 1958 by the master composer Gian Carlo Menotti, with its performances of prose, theatre, film, concerts and exhibitions, represents one of the most prestigious and fashionable international events in the region.

Spoleto. The Cathedral,

Spoleto. The Cathedral. Detail of the facade

Spoleto. The ancient capital of the Longobard duchy at the feet of Monteluco (the sacred mountain), dominated by La Rocca.

Spoleto. Church of San Salvatore, an extremely interesting paleo-Christian building constructed at the end of the IV century or at the beginning of the V, defined the "most important ancient monument in Spoleto".

Spoleto. Church of San Salvatore, detail of the entablature.

Spoleto. Detail of the arches of the gigantesque Ponte delle Torri, a monumental structure (approx. 76 metres high and 230m long) the work of Matteo Gattapone (sec. XIII-XIV).

Spoleto. Church of San Pietro, constructed in the early V century in remembrance of the transportation of Rome of a relic of the saint's chain, and rebuilt between the XII and XIII centuries. The relief work on the facade, carried out in the XII-XIII centuries, is considered, as a whole, the greatest masterpiece of Romanic sculpture in Umbria.

Orvieto

Orvieto stands on a high plain of tufa, 200 metres above the alluvial plain of the Paglia, an is an exceptional example of integration between nature and human intervention. Visiting this town is like passing through history, for here we can find, stratified and concentrated, in a pre-established space, the traces of every époque, for almost three millennia. The cathedral dating back to 1263 is simply breathtaking, doubtlessly the most important architectural statement of the town, with its splendid Gothic facade and wealth of decoration and internal chapels. In the ancient town we can also find the Well of San Patrizio constructed – on the wishes of Pope Clemente VII – in 1528-37 following plans by Antonio da Sangallo the Younger, the Palazzo dei Sette from 1300, the Palazzo del Capitano del Popolo (XII century) and Palazzo Soliano (1262), home to no fewer than two museums: the Museum dedicated to the Cathedral and the Museum of Modern Art. Other monuments of importance include the Teatro Mancinelli (1866), the impressive Underground Town and the necropolis of the Tufa Crucifix, a large cemetery area on the northern slopes sheltered by the tufa rock, and dating back to the Etruscan period. The material which formed the burial objects of the tombs is on display in the National Archaeological Museum (Piazza del Duomo). The visitor should also see the Carlo Faina Museum (opposite the cathedral), hosting the wealthiest collection of Greek ceramics present in Umbria, including Attic vases with black and red figures, Etruscan vases, and also cinerary urns, bronze objects and a rich collection of medals.

Orvieto, constructed over a large tufa platform. The Cathedral, named after Santa Maria Assunta in Cielo, stands out as an outstanding synthesis of architecture and decorative arts.

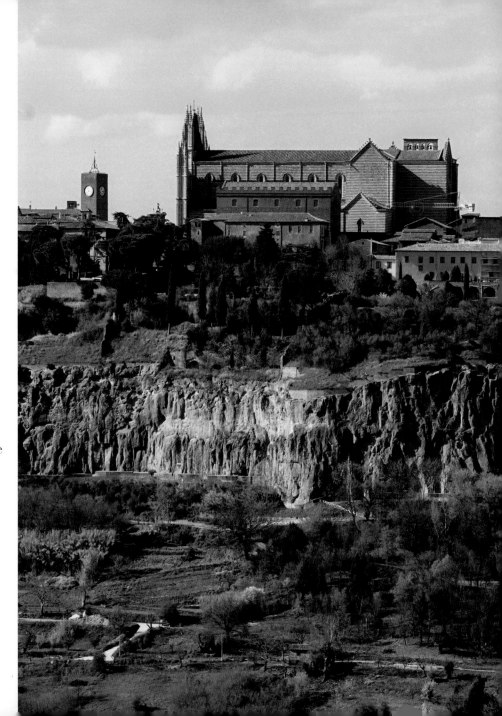

Orvieto. The right side of the Cathedral, in black and white rows .

Orvieto. The vast interior of the Cathedral, with three naves and cylindrical columns.

Orvieto. Palazzo del Capitano del Popolo (detail). A magnificently simple building, of harsh beauty, in the style typical of the early phase of the Free Council (XIII century). It is today used as a Congress Centre.

Orvieto. Market in Piazza del Popolo.

previous page:
Civitella del Lago, ancient hillside village. Panorama over Lake Corbara, created in the 1950s by the construction of a dam on the river Tiber.

Montegiove. La Scarsuola. An ideal city created by Tomaso Buzzi, one of the most important 20th century architects. A free assemblage of monuments from the past, the city includes a group of 7 theatres culminating in an acropolis, a mountain of building one inside the other revealing infinite perspectives, literary suggestions and philosophical references. For the visitor it is like an incipient journey between the sacred city (the ancient Franciscan convent) and the profane city (the theatrical laboratories overloaded with symbols and secrets).

Porano. Castel Ribello (XI century), built on a high plain to dominate the traffic on the ancient Via Cassia.

Vineyards in the area
around Orvieto.

Montecchio.
Panorana.

Terni and the Amerino

Alviano. Panorama.
Characteristic settlement
between hills eroded by ravines
forming an environment of great
beauty, dominated by the
magnificent castle (today Town
Hall) of square plan with corner
towers and Renaissance
courtyard.

Lugnano in Teverina. Church of Santa Maria Assunta, constructed in the second half of the XII century and reorganized in the 15th century; it is one of the most important Romanic churches in Umbria.

Lugnano in Teverina. Church of Santa Maria Assunta, detail of the facade with the rose window.

Narni. Panorama. Town of ancient origins standing on a spur dominating the gorge of the river Nera and the basin of Terni.

Narni Scalo. Surviving arch from the Bridge of Augustus, called so because it was constructed on the occasion of the modernisation of the Via Flaminia, in Augustan times. Approx. 160m long and almost 30m above the level of the waters of the river Nera, it was completely covered with blocks of travertine. Originally with four (or three) arches, it still preserves that on the left intact, while the others were destroyed over time.

Narni Rocca. Impressive construction built in the second half of the 14th century on the wishes of Cardinal Egidio Albornoz. Among the architects who worked on the project were possibly Ugolino I di Montemarte and Matteo Gattapone.

Terni

The second provincial capital of the region, was at the end of the 19th century referred to as the "Italian Manchester", and owes its current fame to the creation of large-scale industries in the last twenty years of the 19th century. These were further augmented in the early years of the 20th century by hydroelectric plants of national importance. Indeed, the installation of the steelworks and later of chemical industries and hydroelectric plants definitively altered the urban-territorial framework of the town. The phase of de-industrialisation over the last few years and the expansion of abandoned areas has once again changed the appearance and functions of the city. In Piazza della Repubblica stands the Town Hall, once of the Podestà, reconstructed in 1878 in Renaissance style by Benedetto Faustini. Corso Tacito was constructed from 1870 to connect the centre with the railway station. Worth visiting, in the 18th century palazzo Gazzoli, is the Municipal Art Gallery named after Orneore Metelli - one of the greatest exponents of naif painting in the XX century. This hosts the most important works of local art between the XIX and XX centuries, with particular reference to the fortunate artistic period of the 1930s, which saw Terni flourish. Terni is also celebrated in Italy and throughout the world for its patron Saint Valentine, "the protector of lovers", celebrated on 14th February every year, the date of his martyrdom. A classic excursion from Terni is to the 'Cascata delle Marmore' waterfalls, formed artificially by the water falling from the river Velino on the high plain of the Marmore into the river Nera. The spectacle of the waterfall is heightened by the roar and the atomising of the water which in certain atmospheric conditions creates highly unusual chromatic effects.

Carsulae. *Roman city founded along the Via Flaminia and developed during the Empire. Tombs and arch of San Damiano and Traiano.*

Terni. The Large Press. Situated in front of the railway station, it is a notable example of industrial archaeology of a very strong visual impact due to its size: 12.000 tonnes, constructed by the Day Brothers, it started working in 1935 and stopped in 1993.

Terni. Detail of the stairway of Casa Briganti (or Pallotta), planned by the architect Mario Ridolfi.

Terni. Scuola "Leonardo da Vinci", planned by Mario Ridolfi. Architectural detail.

Terni. View of the historical centre.

Terni. Church of San Francesco, detail.

following page:
Terni. Panorama of Viale B. Brin
and of the Steelworks.

Cascata delle Marmore (7 km from Terni), one of the most unusual and fascinating spectacles of "nature" celebrated between the 18th and 19th centuries by travellers on the "Grand Tour". It is formed by the falling of the waters of the Velino river into the Nera. Created artificially by the ancient Romans in 271 B.C. to reclaim the plain of Rieti, it was later used for hydroelectric purposes. The bubbly white mass of the waters makes three leaps, covering a total height difference of 165 metres.

Lake Piediluco, situated on the border between Umbria and Lazio. This tranquil lake attracts in particular the lovers of canoeing and rowing, which are also popular on lake Corbara and the upper part of the River Tiber.

Amelia. The surrounding walls in a polygonal form.

Amelia. Panorama. We can just make out the silhouette of the Cathedral and of the polygonal tower.

following page:
The countryside around Giove.

Porchiano. Panorama.

The Valnerina

*Panorama of the Valnerina with
the isolated village of Caso.*

Ferentillo. La Rocca. Ancient dwelling, of probable early medieval construction (VIII century), divided into two castles facing each other on opposing slopes, it formed a powerful barrier across the valley, controlling an important crossroads.

Ferentillo. Church of Santo Stefano. In the crypt, the particular conformation of the ground has made possible a process of mummification of the bodies that had been deposited there. The mummies, with clothes, hair and physiognomy still intact, despite the passage of time, are on display in twenty reliquaries.

San Pietro in Valle. Benedectine Abbey, among the foremost documents of early medieval art in Central Italy. Founded by the Duke of Spoleto Faroaldo in the VIII century, on the site in which the two hermits Lazzaro and Giovanni had lived, it is completely surrounded by the thick and rigorous vegetation which engulfs the entire Valnerina. Extremely important, albeit ruined, are the frescoes of the church representing one of the few examples of early medieval painting.

Vallo di Nera. A typical alley and the bell tower of the Church of Santa Maria.

Panorama of the Valnerina with the isolated village of Cerreto.

Norcia

At 604 m. above sea level, Norcia is 170 km from Rome and 100 km from Perugia. The visitor is struck immediately by its circle of walls, with a characteristic heart shape. It is a town that has undergone continuous transformation caused by numerous earthquakes which have repeatedly struck. It does however manage to preserve precious traces of its past. In the square we find the Basilica of San Benedetto with a crypt of Roman origins, a facade from the XIV century, the bell tower from 1388 and the Portico delle Misure, with the ancient scales in stone for weighing cereal (XVI century). Worthy of note are the Town Hall, with a lower lodge (from the XIV century) and upper lodge and steps from the XIX century; and the Castellina, a monumental four-sided fortress (residence of the mountain prefect) erected on the site of the ancient chapel of Santa Maria Argentea and of the Palazzo del Podestà in the XVI century, following plans by Vignola. Norcia is also famous for its gastronomy. Many typical local products can be found: the delicious black truffles of Norcia, an authentic gem of the Valnerina, the hams and other cold meats, the renowned lentils of Castelluccio (the highest settlement in the Umbrian-Marches Appennines at 1,453m), the farro (spelt wheat) of Monteleone di Spoleto, the trout from the river Nera, mushrooms and fruits of the wood; all of which is embellished by a vast choice of wines.

Norcia. Church of San Benedetto (detail of the facade). Standing to the right of the Town Hall, erected possibly in early medieval times (according to tradition, on the site of the house of the saint's parents), it was rebuilt in 1389 and several times restructured. The facade, belonging to the 14th century building but reconstructed higher up after 1859, has a beautiful Gothic portal with relief on its external arch and wooden shutters from 1578; it is flanked by two elegant niches with the statues of San Benedetto and of his twin Santa Scolastica.

Norcia. Panorama.

Norcia. 'Norcineria' publicising traditional local products.

Norcia. The 'marcite'.

Cascia

Cascia is famous throughout the world for being the birthplace of Santa Rita (1381-1457); it is therefore a well-known destination for religious and environmental tourism. The land of the Municipality of Cascia, including the strip of the Apennine Mountains to the south of the Monti Sibillini, consists mainly of rolling green hills and steep slopes of karstic nature. Roman remains, ruins of castles and medieval towers testify to the ancient origins of Cascia going back to pre-Roman times. The sanctuary of Santa Rita, finished in 1948, besides the primitive church and convent, was started in 1937 and made a basilica by Pio XII in 1955. The complex presents numerous stylistic features (Classical, Byzantine, Gothic) from among which emerge the main altar, a recent work by Giacomo Manzù (1981). In the adjacent monastery of Santa Rita, from the XII century, are to be found the memories of the saint herself: the oratory with the Crucifix, where in 1472 her stigmatization occurred; the 15th century courtyard, with the prodigious vines; the cell preserving her wooden sarcophagus painted in tempera, into which the saint's body was laid in 1457.

Cascia. Classic destination for mass religious tourism due to the presence of the monastery of Santa Rita (native of the nearby Roccaporena).

Preci. Abbey of Sant'Eutizio a Piedivalle. Built in proximity of the caves in which in the VI century hermits coming from Syria took refuge. The church, dating back to 907 but enlarged in 1190, looks over two cloisters and is dominated by a 17th century bell tower constructed on a rocky spur. The exterior is characterised by an original facade with a beautiful Romanic portal and a rose window enclosed in the symbol of the Evangelists.

Altopiano di Castelluccio. The highest and vastest carsick basin on the Umbrian-Marches Apennines, dominated by the chain of the Sibillini culminating in the Mount Vettore.

Altopiano di Castelluccio in bloom.

150

Ancarano. Church of Sant'Antonio. Fresco with San Cristoforo (XIV century).

Ancarano. Remains of the Castle of Castelfranco (XIV century).

Campi. Panorama.

*Campi. Church of San Salvatore,
the rose window.*

printed in July 2008 at the Petruzzi printing office

Note

Note

Note

Note